"This stirring collection moves, as the author puts it in 'Port au Prince,' at 'the sweet, stubborn pace of love and sorrow.' This would be a less persuasive collection if it failed to confront all its sorrows head-on; and yet, by way of scrupulous and ultimately affectionate attention even, say, to 'the unhappy widower who lied to you and yelled at your kids,' it demonstrates that love, divine and human at once, must prevail. One comes away from Davis's book with an assurance available only by grace."

—SYDNEY LEA, Poet Laureate of Vermont

"A lovely collection, filled with calmly spoken words and subtle blessing light."

—DICK ALLEN, Poet Laureate of Connecticut

STILL WORKING IT OUT

The Poiema Poetry Series

Poems are windows into worlds; windows into beauty, goodness, and truth; windows into understandings that won't twist themselves into tidy dogmatic statements; windows into experiences. We can do more than merely peer into such windows; with a little effort we can fling open the casements, and leap over the sills into the heart of these worlds. We are also led into familiar places of hurt, confusion, and disappointment, but we arrive in the poet's company. Poetry is a partnership between poet and reader, seeking together to gain something of value—to get at something important.

Ephesians 2:10 says, "We are God's workmanship . . . ," *poiema* in Greek—the thing that has been made, the masterpiece, the poem. The Poiema Poetry Series presents the work of gifted poets who take Christian faith seriously, and demonstrate in whose image we have been made through their creativity and craftsmanship.

These poets are recent participants in the ancient tradition of David, Asaph, Isaiah, and John the Revelator. The thread can be followed through the centuries—through the diverse poetic visions of Dante, Bernard of Clairvaux, Donne, Herbert, Milton, Hopkins, Eliot, R. S. Thomas, and Denise Levertov—down to the poet whose work is in your hand. With the selection of this volume you are entering this enduring tradition, and as a reader contributing to it.

—D. S. Martin
Series Editor

COLLECTIONS IN THIS SERIES INCLUDE:

Six Sundays toward a Seventh by Sydney Lea
Epitaphs for the Journey by Paul Mariani
Within This Tree of Bones by Robert Siegel
Particular Scandals by Julie L. Moore
Gold by Barbara Crooker
A Word In My Mouth by Robert Cording
Say This Prayer into the Past by Paul Willis
Scape by Luci Shaw
Conspiracy of Light by D. S. Martin
Second Sky by Tania Runyan
Remembering Jesus by John Leax
What Cannot Be Fixed by Jill Peláez Baumgaertner
Still Working It Out by Brad Davis

Still Working It Out

poems

BRAD DAVIS

CASCADE *Books* · Eugene, Oregon

STILL WORKING IT OUT
Poems

The Poiema Poetry Series 13

Cascade Books
An Imprint of Wipf and Stock Publishers
199 W. 8th Ave., Suite 3
Eugene, OR 97401

www.wipfandstock.com

ISBN 13: 978-1-62564-813-6

Cataloging-in-Publication data:

Brad Davis.

Still working it out : poems / Brad Davis.

x + 62 p.; 23 cm

The Poiema Poetry Series 13

ISBN 13: 978-1-62564-813-6

1. American Poetry—21st century. I. Title. II. Series.

PS3562.C8586 2014

Manufactured in the USA.

Cover image: Detail from *Birds Descending through Snow*, by Jessica Scriver. Acrylic and graphite on panel. Used with permission of the artist.

for Deb

Still is the unspoken word, the Word unheard,
The Word without a word, the Word within
The world and for the world

—FROM "ASH WEDNESDAY," SECTION V, BY T. S. ELIOT

Contents

Contents

Acknowledgments

Grateful acknowledgment is made to the editors of the following journals in which this book's poems, sometimes in different form, were first published:

The Adirondack Review: "From the Inside," "July"
Anglican Theological Review: "What I Answered"
Brilliant Corners: "Cecil McBee's Right Ear"
The Cafe Review: "The Guineas of Gardiner Creek"
Chautauqua: "Daylight Savings," "Epithalamion"
The Cresset: "Cosmos," "Easter Sonnet"
DoubleTake: "The Exhibit"
EcoTheo Review: "Gardiner Creek"
Icarus: "Fr. Nicholas" (sections 2, 5, 6, 8)
Image: "Port-au-Prince," "Still Working It Out"
LETTERS: "Return to Coronado"
Michigan Quarterly Review: "On Little Boys & their Guns"
The Paris Review: "In Your Absence," "Simple Enough," "So It Goes,"
    "Washing Dishes After the Feast"
Poetry: "On the Way to Putnam," "Stepping Through Mercury"
Puerto del Sol: "Love Song" (AWP Intro Journal Award)
Relief: "One A.M., Mid-January," "Compost," *"Step away from the
    closing door"*
Ruminate: "Self Portrait w/ Icon," "The Yoke"
St. Katherine Review: "January," "Fr. Nicholas" (section 3)
Spiritus: "Vocation"
Suss: "From Here I Cannot Say What Kind It Is"
Tar River Poetry: "Instant Karma"
Wind: "Time. Coffee. Rain"
Windhover: "Mary"

Acknowledgments

The following poems appeared in the chapbook, *Self Portrait w/ Disposable Camera* (Finishing Line, 2012: finalist for Black River and White Eagle Coffee Store Press chapbook contests): "On Little Boys & their Guns," "Cecil McBee's Right Ear," "Instant Karma," "Simple Enough," "Washing Dishes After the Feast," "In Your Absence," "On the Way to Putnam," "Love Song," "The Exhibit," "Stepping through mercury," *"Step away from the closing door,"* "So It Goes," "Time. Coffee. Rain," "What I Answered," and "Self Portrait."

1

The Exhibit

Over on Lexington, in the glassy foyer
of Saint Peter's Lutheran, four

Fujimura paintings, the largest
a two-panel sea of blues and greens

with—faintly—a fruited quince emerging
or disappearing, like the entire New York skyline

in the holiday blizzard we stepped back into
early that afternoon, threading our way home

around abandoned taxis. Pushing through the best
of the storm's windblown drifts, down each

unplowed block of the graying city,
no more than ten souls in sight—all boots

and mittens, scarves and hats—and finally,
above the intersection we call ours, maybe thirty pigeons

playing mid-air, like children or bundled tongues of flame
not quite ready to complete their ecstatic descent.

If I could, I'd paint it—the appearance
of the likeness of the glory of the Lord—after

late Turner. No borders, no date, no discernible time
of day. Only the relative coordinates:

West 51st Street at 9th Avenue.
Though really it could be almost anywhere.

Time. Coffee. Rain

for JGD

We've not seen such rain for months. And maybe
because of the storm, or what fell from the cheek
of a young girl asleep in Malaysia, Charlie Hunter's
jazzy cover of Marley's *Natty Dread* just leapt
onto the cafe's new stereo. Here on the fat edge

of this window counter, as I relish having scored
a parking space within steps of my weekly coffee stop,
I elect to consider a notion I've heard for decades,
that it's better to enter heaven minus sinful parts
than be thrown undivided into hell. I get a picture

I don't like of me standing at that threshold, various
limbs, organs, glands tagged, "Property of Hell,"
and suddenly I'm aware that neither the prospect
of gaining heaven whole nor the anticipation of shame
at having given hell even the slightest satisfaction

has proved sufficient to effect the good result.
Sure, I'd like to be pure in heart; I'd like to see God,
but these days I'm trying to be kinder to my body.
Besides, tonight after his lesson at Longy, my son and I
are on to hang around the square and, after burritos,

settle ourselves at a front table in a hotel jazz club
to witness firsthand Charlie Hunter's eight-string magic.
I'm holding two tickets for the ten o'clock show,
and if the radio weather man's on target, by the time we
hit the road home this rain should be well out to sea.

Still Working It Out

*for Robin Needham, killed
in the 2004 Christmas tsunami*

Something
shuddered in the un-

fathomable dark, and a wave
shouldered forth

like an eighteen wheeler
skidding sideways

into oncoming traffic—a wave
inhering by the power

of a word lovely
as snow on a navy sleeve,

the same word
that shuddered in each

dark cell of the dead
Christ, a wave shouldering forth

like a new heaven, new
earth, clearing away

the old, the impossible—a wave,
a word, terrible as it is

great, great as it is holy
and terrible.

Love Song

She's always here, the heron, tip-toeing
long shadows through tall grass

and over the spindly gray limbs that litter
the south end of the lake. I cannot

always navigate their tangle to observe
by kayak the slow technique

of the elegant bird, thin neck and head
poking spear-like at the rising moon

to swallow her quicksilver prey.
But I do not come here to see a bird hunt

or watch a moose forage or even one
pair of feasting waxwings dance on air.

I come out, reclined in yellow fiberglass,
to inhabit the instant of last light

suspended between the darkening sky
and water. I come here to remember

how small I am, how nearly
invisible toward midnight I become,

enfolded by the skin of my slender craft.
How I love to all but disappear

when the moon finally sets and what's left
to burn inside this diminutive form

is the faint testimony of ancient stars.

So It Goes

Winter antelopes into erstwhile
      dogmas committed against an ivory
            cane, and three ducats of pilsner

can't buy me lust or you levitating
      with one hand on the other in arcs
            of unctuous radiator steam falling

all over itself like drunken blind luck
      or a dispossessed Carnegie.
            Don't get me wrong. Trains are

my optimal frame of deference,
      their unsung articles gallivanting
            the transvaal with brash gargoyles

in a grand quartersawn wish
      to make moguls of slush piles
            the old-fashioned way, by blowing

in their alabaster nostrils. And reeking
      of time, I am here to report that
            the gossamer intersection of infinite

space and your sizzling flywheel
      has fibrillized a cantaloupe so far out
            of season only a dissociative lemur

would admit to not seeing the humor
      in it. Were this not the case, dear
            other, would I have told you?

Epithalamion

Disconsolate planet, broken
        wheel of a stellar Conestoga,
wild, gorgeous earth

awhirl in a well-
        ordered circle dance,
each body and distance

enamored of strong
        forces and weak, and here
on this farm, on this

evening of your long
        awaited wedding day,
the next well called

step in the reel, reach
        for a partner's hand
is always blind

improvisation, craft
        of memory and the hope
that when your foot descends

a barn floor will be there,
        when the hand closes, another's
will close gladly into yours.

Cosmos

no way of knowing how many there may be

the prime numbers are

God's fingers

and all other numbers are

transparent monofilaments fanning out

from each of God's odd digits

at the frayed ends of which are

all the other things

times and places—every elsewhere all at once

suspended—

even this

thing, *sadness*, and how

far all the numbers are from understanding

On the Way to Putnam

Were you to tell him how,
in late summer's

westering light,
his yellow cornfields and,

toward the middle,
that lone, misshapen tree

had become your very own
Serengeti, complete

with buzzards
ascending and descending

upon some bloated corpse,
likely a wildebeest,

Mr. Amaral, a businessman,
would nod politely.

Vocation

The world is a bright field
and I a laborer

enlisted by a brighter love, a light
delighted to illumine

every curve and canyon,
ice cap and prairie,

the scuffed floor tiles in this
small town cafe, each

face at work or tarrying
here. Like Simone, barista

whom my wife wants our friend
Geoff to meet; or Ian

from Ireland who speaks well
of his Savior to anyone

with time and ears to hear; or kind
Christine who runs the place;

or Ahmed and his chatty band
of schoolmate brothers

whose prophet has no peer.
This is the bright

world, my field, little universe
that I will fail—if I fail

to attend to each part and the whole
and the light that delights

to illumine shop, river, hedgerow,
village and villager.

From Here I Cannot Say What Kind It Is

To fool the cat, a bird
        flails in the grass, feigns
                injury to distract from

actual weakness. Something
        to admire. But for
                go-to-town shirts—

blue to mimic workingman's
        blue—Brecht
                had his tailored in silk.

A different kind of con.
        Like Picasso's ride:
                by all appearances

plebeian, quintessence
        of taxi; in point of fact,
                purely limousine.

Yet what of a simulated mid-
        coital tremble to
                cover a thrilling partner's

poverty of stamina
        or technique? I get dizzy
                trying to sort it all out:

the distance between
        saving another's
                and saving one's own.

Port-au-Prince

Even at escape velocity, we move so slowly, and having escaped, we
walk, run if it suits the moment, always return to walk, a chair, a bed.
So slowly, whether on a park trail or a space station treadmill or from
the room having kissed a child goodnight. We cannot outpace the
sun or moon, the wave that steals over us, the bullet, the adder, the
awful intent of the wicked. Who can flee the home a quake fells in five
seconds? Or having escaped, return to save the child asleep in bed? We
move so slowly in these lovely, supple skins that collision with our kind
while walking is not fatal. Embarrassing, perhaps, or humorous and,
yes, even sexy, suddenly generative, now and then, of gratitude that
we move as we do—so slowly—the sweet, stubborn pace of love and
sorrow.

The Night I Walked Out

of a candlelight service
of Advent lessons and carols, the dour usher
closed the chapel's oak door

behind me, and long-expected
snow, like unvoiced hallelujahs wondrously
crystallized, kissed

my forehead, eyelashes, cheeks—
as if, from out of starless nowhere, love
had become contingent, delicate matter, hallowing

the night.

Daylight Savings

for Erwin

On an island tucked like a crumbling morsel between dissimilar, out-
  facing forks: the historic homestead

Where, well before the sell-offs and high-end development, your
  family kept slaves to work the fields

And keep the manor lovely. Now, what remains of the family's ancient
  holdings there has been passed to you,

And you have heard African voices singing from the soil, choir-like,
  calling among the new plots and rows.

Here, on the shadowed, southeast corner of a siren-crested, mainland
  intersection, traffic slows

For pedestrians, and I consider the invitation, along with neighbors, to
  join you for the first annual

Winter "plant & sing"—garlic and rye—celebration of thanks, bread-
  breaking, and making music through the night.

I like to think you are assembling, at last, the freeman's choral response
  the slaves have been calling for

These past centuries. So much difficult forgiveness to be worked out,
  forgetting nothing, and it may be true:

In your body —aching hips, uninsurable preconditions, slow-dimming
  desires—beats a redeemer's heart,

Ambitious engine of such love as may, like this brief evening's fast-
  fading light, die nevertheless loving.

The Guineas of Gardiner Creek

There's this old Manor, decrepit, ticky,
patrolled by dappled tick-eaters
clawking endlessly their grey, clown-
headed blather—*decay, decay*—senseless
feathered iambs, making endless
rounds around the infested grounds.
They serve and annoy, occasion
an occasional smirk, laugh, dissimilar
verse, make silence sweeter. Ah,
the possibilities they inspire, those petty
red-lipped bleaters—*today, today*—the sun
rising on that ticky, decrepit Manor.
Dappled, senseless, useful, they are
all among themselves happy, most of all.

Gardiner Creek

They who preach the world
is mine to make, exhaust me.

As though without me—or
someone sadly like me—there is

no epic tale of light's procession here,
no narrative of tides

or of desiring birds. Is this
what they, bedside,

tell their children?
Out here, in dawn's half-light,

where the world makes me whole—us
whole—I praise the narrow inlet,

its brackish story, that warbler nearby
getting it said—*I am here.*

2

Fr. Nicholas

All four seasons in that same wool cassock, always at six & slowly,
every weekday morning down the far side of Bay Street, Nicholas
walks through town.

I remember his first boat—we were ten—& the old, twenty-five
horsepower motor his father bought from mine. All spring after
school he worked on it, sanding off the old paint, refitting the seats &
oarlocks, anticipating the rub of rope on gunwale, the first spiny, green
haul of lobster in a boat of his own. For hours, perched on a stump
outside their barn-like garage, I'd watch, & whenever I inquired into
what he was doing, he'd answer, hardly looking up.

All four seasons on each return trip from the bakery by the causeway,
Nicholas cradles a long white bag of hot bread. Dr. Morse, the
pharmacist, tells me I make too much of Father's routine. Says we all
concoct formulas for getting by. I say, while he walks, Father prays
silently for each & every one of us—& every morning as he passes
opposite my rooms above the old five-&-dime, I cross myself.

Devotion, Father's been fond of telling us lately, has more to do with courage than piety, & without fail, I hear again my own father's voice lecturing my mother & me—over Brahms—of passion, sacrifice, & the necessity of routine. I don't think my father ever worried I'd become fearful of him. Still, after each lecture he'd take me for a ride into town to the docks, & we'd watch the gulls hover off the backsides of trawlers. I knew it was my time for asking questions &, on the drive home, ice cream at Bailey's.

I never, till now, doubted Father's word, & even now, it's not that I don't believe it's true. It's that I doubt devotion is anything most of us in the parish have even a passing interest in, like lizards or the southwest. We love the idea of one of us, plain & simple, vested, arms outstretched between brass candlesticks, bearing our world boldly to the throne of grace—& so long as he continues to make us feel welcome, loved & treasured here, he could accomplish nothing else, believe no more than we do, & we'd keep the rectory in good repair forever.

Monday,
Week of the Sunday closest to July 6

As a child I thrived on leather-bound books the size of pulpit Bibles.
I imagined my father the world's authority on such collectibles, & for
years kept completely secret the ritual I watched him perform most
every evening as I tiptoed past the study to the bathroom.

He kept his collection in two large oak & glass cases he bought at
auction the summer the jeweler went bankrupt. Lifting a volume, like
an egg from a nest, he'd set it down on the plush red pillow atop the
counter, adore it as he did my well-rounded mother, & in one smooth,
deliberate motion, bend at the waist until his face, eyes closed, hovered
cloud-like, nose inside an inch of the broad, calfskin plain. Two long,
deep draughts & only then would he straighten, adjust his eyeglasses,
& actually open the thing.

Each morning, for months after he died, I practiced the rite, inventing
gestures of my own over the little red book of prayers & poems
mother'd bought for me & inscribed with a fancy pen—*on the occasion
of your first communion.*

When Nicholas' mother was hospitalized for the last time, I visited her
weekly. Kept her up on the doings around town. Toward the end, once
I knew she couldn't see my father's likeness in my eyes, or hear clearly
my mother's tongue on mine, I asked her—though certainly not before
the usual to & fro of newsy chatter—if her son had ever expressed an
interest in the ladies. I told her, from what I heard tell, the Harris girl'd
been keen on him a while, but she'd never say yes if he never asked. *No,*
she replied softly, *he's never dated.*

After she died, Nicholas halved the number of his lobster pots. Started
splitting the extra time between fixing things for anyone who asked
& heading off upstate every third weekend for what we later learned
were appointments with the bishop. I never did believe the rumors,
& each time he went away, I'd swing by her gravesite Saturdays after
breakfast & set out new flowers, just so, at the foot of that smooth,
pink-ribboned stone he'd ordered special from Italy.

Twenty years ago today Nicholas' mother died. A full five before the
bishop talked him into selling his boat & lobster pots & laying traps
for men. I remember that sermon. The whole town turned out. Priests
from all up & down the state rolled in to lay their hands on him.
Yanked him into orders, just like that. You should have seen his face
pinch in the receiving line when an old, leaf-dry deacon knelt down
right then & there to beg of him his first priestly blessing. Only priest I
ever met who makes robes look manly.

His first couple months as pastor were (I shouldn't say it, but it's a
matter of public fact) fun for us. The bishop hadn't required him to go
away for seminary. Said his age & the parish situation qualified him
for an exemption that, in this case, he was more than happy to grant.
So when it came time for Father's first mass, he swung the incense
like he was throwing a buoy overboard. Had us all in stitches with his
awkward cadences & muffled cusses each time he lost his place. No
question, the acolytes had the hardest go of it. But by Christmas we'd
grown accustomed to him, & by Easter, I couldn't imagine anything
sweeter than taking the Body on my tongue from his large, right hand.

THURSDAY,
WEEK OF THE SUNDAY CLOSEST TO AUGUST 3

Nicholas learned how to work wood from keeping those pots, but it gave me pause last Saturday afternoon. I was letting the dog run when I came upon a small, glass-faced cabin the parish secretary later told me Father'd built for personal retreats in the wooded, northeast corner of the church property. The door had no lock that I could see, so I entered.

The room was spare. A kneeler at the center faced out through the plate glass. A leather Bible open to Ecclesiastes lay beside a journal on a lectern. Against the north wall, an eye-level platform bed, desk & chair directly beneath, & in between, chiseled in caps across a three-foot length of oiled cedar & mounted on the knotty pine wall, *Create in Me a Clean Heart, O God.*

Like a child in a neighbor's tree fort, I don't remember breathing, & left without disturbing a thing.

WEDNESDAY EVENING,
WEEK OF THE SUNDAY CLOSEST TO AUGUST 10

A windless heat wave landed on us yesterday, & Mother's words ring
in my ears: *Until the weather breaks, shop early & keep purchases to a
minimum.* So I shopped this morning for the three-speed window fan
cooling me as I write. Then tomorrow, up to Boston. Asked for these
days back in June, so heat or no heat, I'm city-bound. Good news:
the radio says storms will bring relief over the weekend. Had the car
washed & gassed—all set for an early departure. Mustn't forget, on the
way home, to pick up a present for Nicholas—his fiftieth—& speaking
of our priest, from where I sit, it seems he's gone missing. Dr. Morse
says I'm overreacting. Maybe so. Either way, I really must get some
sleep. The new fan should help.

AUGUST 15,
FEAST OF ST. MARY THE VIRGIN

Wednesday a week ago, after three days not seeing him over breakfast
& before leaving for Boston, I called around. Best I could tell, I was
the first to raise the question of his whereabouts. Not even the parish
secretary thought anything of it.

Thursday the harbor master left a long message on my machine: said
Monday at dawn he'd taxied Nicholas out to the *Sursum Corda* &
watched from the dock the tidy ketch tack neatly into mist beyond the
chop. Mondays are Father's day off. Said he remembered him mumble
something about a mystic center in mercy, like it were a destination
Down East or something—which is when my machine cut him off.

Sunday the diocese sent a priest on holiday from the Midwest to read
the liturgy. After the sermon, I slipped out through the side door of the
nave & made for the little cabin behind the fellowship hall.

Yesterday Dr. Morse offered me a job at the pharmacy to keep his
books & pay the bills—& I began taking flowers to Nicholas' mother's
grave again. He never did get used to us calling him Father.

Every morning at breakfast, to remind me whose I am, I still cross
myself. He'll be back. Then, one day when he needs me, when he asks
for me by his bedside, I'll be there for him, like I've always been, from
the beginning—& I'll touch everything.

3

Return to Coronado

The ferry's a bridge now, lined
with signs advertising suicide
prevention by cell phone. I was
almost delivered on that ferry, Bev
in labor, their car loaded on first
to be the first off—the hospital
at the North Island naval base
gone now, too, where they, like
a flight deck crew, landed me days
before Graham sailed for Korea.

It's been over fifty years,
but I am back for a weekend,
unexpectedly grateful for having
not been born elsewhere, where
there are no oil-slick sea lions
lounging on bell buoys, or mile-long
parades of sailboats setting out
from and returning to harbor. No
City College Jazz Fest, towering
palms, or brown-faced pelicans
doing their prehistoric best
from off-limit Navy dock pilings.

Here in Coronado, by a concrete
bench near a sand volleyball court,
on any clear morning like this,
one could easily forget that
you cannot serve both the carrier-
sized flag at the base's main gate
and the Lamb whose players, from
a small, Orange Avenue stage,
raise no banner but His. And that,
born to choose between these

allegiances, I must re-cross
the tempting bridge, board
a jet for Connecticut, and prove
this day whom I say I serve.

Quietly

The snow continues to fall.
When she joins me
I will build a fire we will keep
through the afternoon
into evening. This is how we live.
The logs will burn down;
she will grade exams on the couch;
I will read Wendell Berry
or the Iliad or finish a new
song I've been revising
since the turn of the year.
It really is like this.
If we go out for dinner,
it will be with friends
whose daughter just had a baby,
no self-conscious flourishes
of cleverness, no
flamboyant posing as avant-garde.
Our lives have meaning
we do not make for ourselves,
or have to. It is a gift,
like the falling snow and this time
to get our work done.

One A.M., Mid-January

The rate of raw data increase,
        number of blog posts per second—
                who keeps up? It's like trying

to monitor each cell dividing
        in the infant curled in my arms
                or to account for the variations

between snowflakes burying
        our car. Driven by the fear
                of falling too far behind, I read

what I've time and patience for,
        calculate implications, incredulous
                at how little makes any difference

for how we live or how
        one stops oneself from shaking
                a screaming, colicky child. Outside,

above the car's disappearing lines,
        the shape of a sequined gown
                suspends from a street light.

I listen to my daughter's
        cat-like breaths. Asleep at last—
                her fingers gripping and releasing

the blue quilt's damp hem.

Toby

In a hole in the orchard
where your family
buries pets,

you bury Toby, stuffed
in a black, biodegradable
plastic bag. Unable

to tell his golden head
from tail and unwilling
to frisk the shapeless package

to locate his snout, you
stoop and center the slimy
tennis ball atop the bag.

You want him, when
he wakes, to smell
your scent on the ball

before bounding off who
knows where. Or with whom.
Now you feel Egyptian,

thinking Toby needs more
than a ball for the journey—needs
rawhide chews, bowls full

of his favorite canned food,
that ratty old blanket. And, yes,
an attendant, maybe one

of your pretty daughters
to wake with him
and make sure he's happy there.

But the ball must suffice. So,
after laying a broad
flagstone shelf atop shapeless

Toby and the ball, you
refill the hole, finishing off
your ancestral work

in the close company of
past pets and early evening's
feral stillness.

Easter Sonnet

The cat is not here.
She has risen

from the cushion
of her favorite chair

where fur lies in clumps
like grave clothes,

the cushion now a reliquary
I cannot revere

and also hope to please
a persnickety spouse.

I know, I know,
this ought not be

even a minor crisis.
But the cat is not here.

Stepping Through Mercury

You have seen my heart, you said
as the glassy vision shook, splintered,
and reassembled into a recognizable
you, stepping toward me as if through
mercury or a sheer, silver wash of water.
In the dream, and clinging to a thin,
dissolving sense of what it was I saw,
I turn and slip away from you, summoned
by another voice, also yours, calling me
to the back porch to witness pollen rise
in waves off the meadow. *A sign,* you'd say,
visible certain mornings in late spring,
the air grown fidgety with impatience,
the angle of the light, just so.

July

A stone patio,
a hummingbird's

whir—the seen
and unseen—fill me

and I am not
the heavier for it.

I bear, beyond
these summer cottons,

only light, a memory
of light, images

of the weighted real
fading out or

into ideas, arguments
durable as the words

framing them.
Like these that I

pass to you—all of July
in a blur of wings.

Compost

Among the old beech's west-running roots,
we spill out, from sink-side plastic containers,
leftover vegetable guts, loam-dreaming
occult microbial transformations
and next summer's tomatoes and basil.

At least once a week one of us makes the trip
across the yard we share with our neighbors
to deposit the goods and, with their well-
tuned pitchfork, turn it over, our work in praise
of worms and dirt. And today I'm thinking

this is why we drove 9th Avenue downtown
from West 51st Street toward the steaming pile
of what was left over from the towers' fresh,
flesh-mingled collapse—and though we
could have made it farther, we turned west

at Houston, past SWAT teams and armored
vehicles, then north on West Side Drive into
that parade of twisted metal body parts splayed
on flatbed after flatbed headed for the instant,
plein air morgue on Staten Island. All

the way to the bridge, thousands turned
out to applaud the truck drivers' strange, pall-
bearing work, and crawling north with them,
we were interlopers among those
just doing their jobs—we in the city only

to pick up our musician-son and return him
a few days to his bed in Connecticut.
But he, knowing better somehow that
music would soon serve to raise the city's
dead neighborhoods, stayed behind, in his own

way loam-dreaming transformations, any
number of nonpaying gigs he would lend his
love and anger to, since, regardless of our
odd thing for dark tourism, death must not
have the last word—*is* not the last word.

Cloister

Encircle me.
Won't you

close around
closer than

harbor, paddock,
garden wall—

close as warm
water, folds

of flesh firm
as prayer.

Draw me, love,
to you—

as glad to hold as I
to be held.

Self Portrait w/ Icon

This shed, a three-season studio, these
heavy eyelids. Here, an icon
reads me, tattered image, of a cloth
with dark matter and that
cardinal in the Rose of Sharon I hear
but cannot see. What is more:
a dragonfly or the shadow of one? This
icon spies me entire—sin and loose-
cobbled sanctity—morning to morning
welcomes me whole, and so
where I work I am the work worked over
by a grace as beyond me as I to these
cramped letters here. In the icon,
three sister angels at table
take counsel for the world, for every
habitation, grand or found or piecemeal,
and for the heavy-lidded son
of a wandering Aramean for whom it is
far better and sadder to be here than he can bear.

The Yoke

Neither a chocolate egg's yellow heart
nor the sorry punch line for a set-up
I've long forgotten: *Get the yoke?* But
a handmade thing whose name shares
a semantic bed with Sanskrit *yuga*—body
of instruction caring less for sculpted
postures than a way to align one's life
with liberating wisdom. *Take my yoke
upon you.* Noun metaphor, assuming
specific knowledge and eyes to see
an ancient harness fit for tilling fields,
transporting families, hauling bales,
or, in an emperor's parade, mocking
prisoners marked as beasts of burden.
My yoke is easy, my burden light. Count on
him to play the irony card: hard artifact
of servitude as emblem of freedom.
See him saying this to any two followers,
one on each side, held close, his dark
carpenter arms laid across their shoulders—
I no longer call you servants, but friends.
See him grab firmly to himself those two
fiery sons of thunder and subdue them
with a word of peace; see him fold
his infinite wings around the despairing
pair on their way to Emmaus, and around
the Marys, the inconsolable, the least.

Mary

Mark 14:1–11

The olive grove,
inheritance
and burden, and
she has learned
to read
the breezes
for rain or frost.

The teacher's voice
is a breeze,
and her
grove's oil
is insufficient for
his head
and beard. So

she has bartered
for an
alabaster jar
of nard, not
knowing what
he knows, or how
few his days.

This day,
she wakes to
chattering sparrows.

How to Wait for the Second Coming

Dust and vacuum, because the light
is already here. Between shaking out

this throw rug and that, reverence
the forsythia. Sounds crazy, but bake

rounds of shortcake for the neighbors.
Tie a blue ribbon on the one

you will give to the unhappy widower
who lied to you and yelled at your kids.

At work, spend equal time
with random coworkers and breathe

slowly, savoring each breath the way
you savor each course of a holiday meal.

This is the gift he sends before he comes.

What I Answered

for DLD

It was, of course, the cancer that killed her.
She and I were alone in the hospital room.
You were at the nurses' station, I think,
or in the bathroom, or picking up lunch.
The sun was bright through the window.
We were holding hands and I had just said
something about God. Or faith. Or maybe
about Schuller, or catching the closing night
of a Graham crusade on the tube. In any case,

I had spoken from my love for her, and you know
how I loved her, how easily we laughed together.
Her next words to me were clear and soft.
The tone of her voice, natural. Even calm.
I believe she wanted to know: *Am I dying?*
Yes. It never occurred to me to say anything else.
Besides, she always could see through a lie.
She looked over at me, then away at the window.
Slowly she closed her eyes, squeezed my hand.

No one had prepared me for that silence.
I'll never forget the time she told me how
she enjoyed bragging to her customers
at the laundromat about her daughter being
married to a priest, and how it never failed to raise
their thick, French Catholic eyebrows. I don't
remember wearing my collar to the hospital that day.
Or why I have taken so long to tell you this.
She and I sat there in the bright room holding hands.

4

From the Inside

Picture a room, the walls entirely
of glass, large as a planet, full
of seasons, lakes, forests,
tides, towns and cities, and
where door and doorjamb kiss,

no light or shadow, seamless
as a wall, no knob or hinge—
I passed into this room
through that door, and it closed
behind me with a click

I took for a snapping twig,
and spinning around to see
who or what followed me in,
there was no one, nothing
but a stand of ancient

hemlocks in the corner of a yard.
The ways in, as innumerable
as the places we arrive—
and here we are, you and I
in this mid-sized city

facing each other across
an intersection, waiting for
a light to change, a beep
to launch into its permissive
rhythm. And what else? What next?

In Your Absence

I sit. She cooks.
It's not what it looks like.
But then, what does it look like?
Is she pretty?
How old am I?

She cooks. I think
creole, barbeque, stir fry, anything
at all other than what you'd be eating
with me tonight at this counter
in this small town.

What does it look like
now? A man, a woman, a roadside diner.
It's all so damn small from the moon!
Remember? We woke up
that morning—men were on the moon,

and that photograph, "earthrise,"
right there, front page—remember?
They were your words: *so damn small.*
So damn perfect—that photograph
tore my world to confetti.

Across the counter she waits. I think
I'll say it: *The usual.* (New England boiled dinner
with milk and a side of onion rings.)
For one. As always,
she cooks. I remember.

Simple Enough

In my home we take turns with the remote
and whoever's turn it is calls the show.

Rule two: a change of turn must occur
on the half-hour at the commercial break.

If there's a question of whose turn is next
the clicker always travels clockwise.

What more is there to know? We speak
in tongues. We live nowhere near the water.

Where am I going with this?
I'm holding the remote and it's my call.

If someone would write it I'd read cover
to cover *The Sociology of Druthers.*

But I'm stalling. Silence and glossolalia
come easier to me than this posturing,

this fidgeting with the clicker. Last night
I dreamt of falling into snow.

January

for Gray Jacobik

Some blue mornings, fall or spring, the dismal day
rips along countless migratory perforations,
the loud, insufferable geese coming and going
every which way as if they have lost entirely
        their small-brained bearings.

This morning, meaningless nature delivered:
three Canada geese in the whole winter sky,
and I made meaning of it—saw the hollow-boned as
aeroglyph strung behind an invisible biplane
        trailing a banner south—

and it encouraged me, who thinks far too often
of failing, falling from the small place
I have made for my miserable self and dying alone,
a senile bother for the unfortunate intern
        who must attend to me.

There is no comfort. I should know better.
But that clamorous ellipsis! Muscular, banking
into the January wind, their—dare I say it, Gray—
conversation robust, timely and to the point,
        in some small-brained way.

Wearing the Ashes

Out my first floor office window,
Virginia looks the way I feel:
*Who needs this job in this weather
at this time of day?* Up long hours

before the sun, she slaves for a
private school—vacuums the library,
cleans the admissions office toilet.
Schlep does not begin to tell

the story of her sulk across
the parking lot where she drags
her slumped body and a large black
garbage bag. If you knew

I was going to say *garbage bag*,
then maybe you know Virginia, too.
This morning it does me good
to see her reach the lot's far side

and not just place the bag on
the snowy curb but throw it there,
as though it holds the warm, severed
head of her supervisor, and she could not

care less on this Ash Wednesday
whether a garbage truck carts it off
or feral cats ferret out his thick tongue
and make a mid-winter feast of it.

On Little Boys & Their Guns

One internet game engages as many
players as are logged-on and staring into
separate monitors in separate time zones—
splits combatants into two platoons ranging
real-time through a cyber-maze of courtyards
and passageways until one team is terminated,
dispatched by handgun, assault rifle, missile
launcher. Could it be our best and safest
domestic strategy: to permit these units
their virtual death matches, take-no-prisoner
human targeting games, and thereby keep
the short-fused gamers off the streets,
out of the mainstream and honing those
feather-touch motor skills required to pilot
a drone or drive a tank? Haven't recent studies
confirmed that nature, by denying some
their full hormonal birthright, supplies us
with warriors, the tightly-wound, aggressive
type the rest of us know to steer clear of,
trusting God or the fragile rule of law?
Understatement be damned, these players
are out to win, and to kill well is to win big.
A far cry from shivering alone beneath
the Brinker's rhododendron, rain dripping
from the rim of a camouflaged bike helmet,
and out there an unseen enemy patrol fearing
my smooth, triggerless oak branch, the pine
cone grenades crammed in my pockets.

Cecil McBee's Right Ear

On day trips in and out of New York City, we would gaze
across the Hudson at the Jersey palisades,
mother driving, lauding the morning, then evening mist,
our Connecticut sensibility unable to conceive of anything at all

good coming from that Newark-stained Nazareth.
We would not have believed it had we been told
by Leonard Bernstein himself that half his Philharmonic
tunneled daily to and from their work, or that

right there in Englewood, a recording engineer from Hackensack
named Rudy was changing the aural shape of the long-playing world.
It strikes me now that on June 14, 1965, I may have
cast a casual glance across the murky river

at the exact moment Rudy Van Gelder hit the control
room light switch to prep the gear for the Blue Note session
I'm finally hearing, thirty-five years later—
Shorter, Hancock, Chambers, McBee. It's true,

I'm a latecomer to jazz, with more lost ground to cover
than time to cover it, but I've a mind
to cut my losses and lean my whole body into this
grace—this gift of listening—as though the music were just

arriving from the same future Cecil had dialed into back then,
one ear bent on four thick strings and unavailable
to Frank Wolff's Pentax; the other, his right one,
opening out to high hat, piano, saxophone, the camera's lens,

and our Ford Falcon station wagon passing on the far shore.
In the passenger seat, I am twelve years old
humming along to Cousin Brucie's top-forty countdown,
as though a small, sad life might evaporate without it.

Instant Karma

Like a wool-capped and baggy cadre
of skateboarders cruising the fountain
in the cruciform heart of an upscale
suburban mall, seven lanky wasps
just blew in under my back porch roof,
all swoop, glide and bluster, wilding
in this summer-like last day of March.
And whether I freeze or dart
for the door, they have my attention
effectively divided seven ways, fear
and scorn mixing it up with that familiar
flash of panic I am able usually to coast
through en route to normal: the sixty
firm beats per minute I once, in algebra,
slow-breathed down to thirty-two.
Back then I was the kid with attitude,
the WASP who, every day for months,
posted on the board outside the head-
master's office anonymous traces
of a hostile, underground, koanic wit
and made my comrades swear by all
the smoke in a nickel bag never
to turn state's evidence, no matter
the smiling assurances of leniency
tendered by the dean. But it never came
to that. The powers never panicked.
We flew on to college, therapy, careers—
and just now all hope of a quick return
to normal here on the porch has been
dashed, as those original lanky skaters
have been joined by an edgy trio
of black and yellow hornets, a union
of forces logic deems prudent to elude.

Washing Dishes After the Feast

It frightens me to think, she said, interrupting
my holiday banter. Imagining the phrase
as antecedent to a rare gift of honest exchange
between grownup siblings, I dashed
into the split-second of dead air, anticipating silently
her elaboration—*what a mess we've made of things*
for our kids; how many parents of starving
children must hate us for our amazing prosperity
and self-indulgence.
                            But I had misread
her punctuation, took the period as a pause, and all
at once found myself, like that coyote
we used to pull for on Saturday mornings, utterly
without purchase, eyeballing an abyss.
Which is when, glancing back across the divide
of the double sink at her busy hands, I saw her
as though she were curled in a ball on the lip
of a cliff, knees tight to her chest, face buried
in the cotton folds of a holly-green dress.
It's okay, I wanted to tell her. *It scares me, too.*
But I was already plummeting, tumbling in free-fall
to a sunbaked canyon floor, the crazy cur
in her endless cartoon of an unreliable universe.

Self Portrait w/ Disposable Camera

Pemaquid, Maine

Like obsidian planets set in buoyant flesh,
their great round eyes encircled our rented kayaks.
Unlike sharks, *Phoca vitulinae* are not all business.
Admirable for how they subsume necessity
within a will to play, the dozen or so harbor seals
took turns ducking down, then resurfacing,
each time closer, more coy.
                                    The moon that evening
rounded also toward us, fixed in its flight path
and sightless as the lens in the disposable
waterproof camera we passed between our huddled
crafts with vows to send copies when the prints returned.
I am in one of them, two harbor seals off my stern,
beneath me the unaffected arc of the Atlantic.

"Step away from the closing door"

with a nod to Charles Williams

The digitized voice does not threaten, but it is
male, imperative, unlike the female voice
immediately preceding, softer, knowing both
the next and final stops along the subway line.
The door will not stand open forever,
the train must roll on.
                    Here, under the avenues,
the Holy Ghost works overtime, ventriloquist
and self-effacing architect of a traveler's
peace of mind. And it works. The doors close.
The journey continues without incident ten
thousand times daily.
                    But you do not
need to be an habitué of urban bustle
to marvel at the grace of deferring
to disembodied messages. In rural Connecticut,
an hour or so before midnight, a timer turns
all intersection stoplights into cautionary
blinking ones. And motorists get it. Comply. Proceed.

Hanami

for SMP

Of the flowering trees left standing
when, years back,

a parking lot went in,
Look, a neighbor to his son,

Cherry blossoms!
His wife is from Japan.

Their child, a world removed
from her home city

and the holiday
when her family welcomes a rain

of infinite cherry petals
to their festive picnic blanket.

The neighbor knows
that I know that he knows

the loosing blossoms are crabapple.
So I know too there's no

need to set a record straight,
as he and I watch

their lithe son gambol
to catch a cherry petal on his tongue.